A woman is the full circle.
Within her is the power to create,
nurture, and transform.

— Diane Mariechild

Blue Mountain Arts®

Bestselling Titles

By Susan Polis Schutz:

To My Daughter, with Love, on the Important Things in Life

To My Son with Love

By Douglas Pagels:

30 Beautiful Things That Are True About You

42 Gifts I'd Like to Give to You

100 Things to Always Remember... and One Thing to Never Forget

May You Always Have an Angel by Your Side

To the One Person I Consider to Be My Soul Mate

Is It Time to Make a Change?

by Deanna Beisser

I Prayed for You Today

To the Love of My Life

by Donna Fargo

Anthologies:

Always Believe in Yourself and Your Dreams

For You, My Daughter

Friends for Life

Hang In There

I Love You, Mom

I'm Glad You Are My Sister

The Joys and Challenges of Motherhood

The Language of Recovery

Marriage Is a Promise of Love

Teaching and Learning Are Lifelong Journeys

There Is Greatness Within You, My Son

Think Positive Thoughts Every Day

Thoughts to Share with a Wonderful Teenager

True Wealth

With God by Your Side ...You Never Have to Be Alone

You're Just like a Sister to Me

$\mathcal{I}$deals for Women to Live By

Words of Wisdom
to Inspire Meaning and Purpose
in the Daily Lives of Women

Edited by Patricia Wayant

Blue Mountain Press ™
Boulder, Colorado

We wish to thank Susan Polis Schutz for permission to reprint the following poems that appear in this publication: "This life is yours..." and "Many people go from one thing...." Copyright © 1978, 1979 by Continental Publications. And for "If you know yourself well...," "You cannot listen to what...," "Successful People Have Twelve Qualities in Common," and "Sometimes you may think...." Copyright © 1979, 1982, 1986 by Stephen Schutz and Susan Polis Schutz. All rights reserved.

Library of Congress Control Number: 2005905354
ISBN: 1-59842-070-4

ACKNOWLEDGMENTS appear on page 64.

Certain trademarks are used under license.
BLUE MOUNTAIN PRESS is registered in U.S. Patent and Trademark Office.

Printed in the United States of America.
First Printing: 2006

 This book is printed on recycled paper.

This book is printed on fine quality, laid embossed, 80 lb. paper. This paper has been specially produced to be acid free (neutral pH) and contains no groundwood or unbleached pulp. It conforms with all the requirements of the American National Standards Institute, Inc., so as to ensure that this book will last and be enjoyed by future generations.

Blue Mountain Arts, Inc.

P.O. Box 4549, Boulder, Colorado 80306

Ideals for Women to Live By

- Take Time Each Day to Remember What's Important
- Fill Your Life with the Things That Matter Most
- Be the Person You Are Meant to Be
- Strong Women Hold Their Heads High
- Always Be True to Yourself
- Worry Never Solves Anything
- Measure Success in Your Own Way
- Have at Least One True Friend
- Share Your Special Talents and Gifts with the Ones You Love
- Be Accepting of Yourself and Others
- Don't Ever Stop Reaching and Growing
- Learn from Your Mistakes
- Be Enthusiastic About Your Life and Your Work
- Happiness Comes from Within
- Listen to Your Heart
- Beauty Isn't Found Just in Magazines
- Appreciate Your Own Self-Worth
- Be Loving, Compassionate, and Kind
- Find Something to Be Grateful for Every Day
- Perfection Is a Goal, Not a Reality
- Live Your Life Fully
- Stay Positive!
- You Always Have Choices
- Leave the World a Little Better Than You Found It
- Remember All That It Means to Be a Woman
- You're Never Too Old to Make a Difference
- Look for a Little Happiness in Each Day
- Don't Let Anything Stand in the Way of Your Dreams
- Above All Else, Believe in Yourself

Take Time Each Day to Remember What's Important

Take time each day to look at your life with thankfulness and as a gift to enjoy.

Look back on your past with an attitude of appreciation for all the lessons that you've learned and a sense of gratitude as you remember every experience. Don't let regrets trouble you and try to steal your joy, for even less-than-positive experiences teach us lessons and help to shape who we are.

Look to the future and know that for every question not yet answered and every dream not yet realized, there is a tomorrow that will hold you gently in its arms and create the perfect way to make your dreams come true.

And for the rest of your life, know that with love, acceptance, peace, and satisfaction, you will reach every goal you set for yourself and do all the things that you want to do.

— Donna Fargo

Fill Your Life with the Things That Matter Most

Cheer to greet you each morning, so each new day will help you believe that you are one step closer to your dreams.

Peace in your inner being, so you can breathe easy and enjoy every moment of your life.

Faith to encourage and inspire you; to comfort you and heal your hurts; to commune with and be one with; to help you get in touch with your true self.

Laughter to bring you happiness and fun and keep your joy alive; to remind you that life is too short to spend it crying.

<u>Beauty</u> to fill your eyes with the simple gifts that nature brings.

<u>Confidence</u> to do all the things that your true self desires; to conquer your fears and be free to reach your goals.

<u>Friendships</u> that are lasting and true with people who respect your values and are full of sharing and caring.

<u>Memories</u> that are warm and comforting, that you can reflect on and smile, and that last a long while.

— Jacqueline Schiff

Be the Person
You Are Meant to Be

Don't ever be afraid to be who you are. Don't keep yourself from expressing love, kindness, and patience. Don't cut yourself off from the things that nourish your soul. Live in the spirit of life; there are no walls to keep you captive. You are as beautiful as you choose to be.

Take a step you have not dared to take before, a stride in a new direction. Discover a new creation within yourself. When you think you have reached an end, watch for life to take a turn and renew itself. Be victorious in the way you respond to everything that happens to you. Live on the great ocean of possibilities, and sail away toward your dreams.

— Tanya P. Shubin

This life is yours
Take the power
to choose what you want to do
and do it well
Take the power
to love what you want in life
and love it honestly
Take the power
to walk in the forest
and be a part of nature
Take the power
to control your own life
No one else can do it for you
Nothing is too good for you
You deserve the best
Take the power
to make your life
healthy
exciting
worthwhile
and very happy

— Susan Polis Schutz

Strong Women Hold Their Heads High

Strong women are those
who know the road ahead
will be strewn with obstacles,
but they still choose to walk
it because it's the right one
for them.

Strong women are those who
make mistakes, admit to them,
learn from those failures,
and then use that knowledge.

Strong women are easily hurt,
but they still extend their
hearts and hands, knowing
the risk and accepting the
pain when it comes.

Strong women are sometimes
beat down by life, but they
still stand back up and step
forward again.

Strong women are afraid. They face the fear and move ahead to the future, as uncertain as it can be.

Strong women are not those who succeed the first time. They're the ones who fail time and again, but still keep trying until they succeed.

Strong women face the daily trials of life, sometimes with a tear, but always with their heads high as the new day dawns.

— Brenda Hager

Always Be
True to Yourself

Be true to your dreams, and keep them alive. Never let anyone change your mind about what you feel you can achieve. Always believe in yourself.

Be true to the light that is deep within you. Hold on to your joy for life. Keep good thoughts in your mind and good feelings in your heart. Keep love in your life, and you will find the love and light in everyone.

Be giving, forgiving, patient, and kind. Have faith in yourself. Be your own best friend, and listen to the voice that tells you to be your best self.

Be true to yourself in the paths that you choose. Follow your talents and passions; don't take the roads others say you must follow because they are the most popular. Take the paths where your talents will thrive — the ones that will keep your spirits alive with enthusiasm and everlasting joy.

Most of all, never forget that there is no brighter light than the one within you. Keep on being true to yourself. Keep shining your light on others so they will have a reason to smile. Follow your inner light to your own personal greatness, and remember that you are admired and loved just as you are.

— Jacqueline Schiff

Ideals to Live By...

Worry Never Solves Anything

It isn't wise to worry,
and yet at times we all do.
We look uncertainly into the future
and wonder what it holds.
We focus on the problems at hand
instead of the solutions.
Rather than fear "what might be,"
we need to remember that
there are many steps we can take
to create the best for us
and make tomorrow
a place full of promise.

Next time you start to worry,
stop and remember
that if you're doing all you can,
being all you're meant to be,
and trying with all your heart...
then you are on the right path
to a better tomorrow.

— Barbara J. Hall

Sometimes we move the earth,
and sometimes it seems to
move around us.

As you rise to the challenges
of each new day, remember that
the day will come as it should.

Worrying will not prevent today
and will only impede tomorrow.

There are situations we can
control and those we cannot.

Forge ahead with your ideas
and plans, for anything thought
out is worthy.

See yourself as you are: a
viable, intelligent person with
great potential!

— Dana Smith-Mansell

Measure Success
in Your Own Way

Success means something different
  to each one of us,
but it comes to those
  who are willing to work hard
and who continue to be dedicated
  to making their dreams come true.

Success means setting goals
and focusing yourself
in the right direction
  in order to reach them.
It means believing in yourself
  and constantly reminding yourself
that you are capable of achieving
  your desires.

But most of all,
success is being who you are
and feeling proud of yourself
  for every task and challenge
that you face and conquer
  along the way.

— Dena Dilaconi

Successful People Have
Twelve Qualities in Common

They have confidence in themselves
They have a very strong sense of purpose
They never have excuses for not doing something
They always try their hardest for perfection
They never consider the idea of failing
They work extremely hard toward their goals
They know who they are
They understand their weaknesses
    as well as their strong points
They can accept and benefit from criticism
They know when to defend what they are doing
They are creative
They are not afraid to be a little different
    in finding innovative solutions
        that will enable them to achieve their dreams

                             — Susan Polis Schutz

Have at Least One True Friend

The heart needs friendship to make us feel that we belong in life. We need special people who accept us just as we are, who make us laugh when we need to, who cry with us when we're sad, who celebrate with us when we're up, and who are there for us when we're down.

We need people in our lives with whom we can share our everyday thoughts, form a bond, and grow old. We need give-and-take relationships so we can know that there are people we can trust and people with whom we can share a lasting relationship.

We need allies and favorite people who won't desert us and on whom we can really depend — people to stand in for family members who aren't there sometimes. We need friends with whom we exchange favors, who bear with us the boredom of life and share with us its joys.

— Donna Fargo

It's so easy for women
    to slip into self-doubt
          and feeling inadequate.
After all,
we shoulder a lot of responsibilities —
    being supportive of our mates,
    nurturing our children,
    staying in touch with extended family,
    holding down jobs
    while holding down the fort at home.

No wonder we sometimes feel
    anxious, exhausted, and insecure.

We need to know
    we're not alone.
We need to hear
    that other women
    share our experiences.
We need reassurance
    that there's someone who understands —
someone who's been there, done that.

As women, we take turns
    encouraging, supporting,
          and cheering one another on.

                                        — BJ Gallagher

Share Your Special Talents
and Gifts with the Ones You Love

Many people
go from one thing
to another
searching for happiness
but with each new venture
they find themselves
more confused
and less happy
until they discover
that what they are
searching for
is inside themselves
and what will make them happy
is sharing their real selves
with the one they love

— Susan Polis Schutz

Where Love Grows

Love grows in a garden
where a grandmother with arthritic hands
weeds vegetables, strawberries, and rhubarb
to feed her husband who has forgotten
    her once-lovingly-said name.

Love grows in a bedroom
as a mother finishes the chapter
    of a cherished book
while tucking in a sleepy child.

Love grows on a bleacher
while proud parents watch a son
run three yards before getting buried
    by the opposing team.

Love grows in a kitchen
as tired hands stir the "soup of the day"
to feed those who are too beaten
    by this world
to have a home of their own.

Love grows on this earth
in every heart, every person, and every soul
touched by the miracle of being human.

— Faith Tomassacci

Be Accepting of Yourself and Others

Acceptance means that you
  can find the serenity within
to let go of the past
  with its mistakes and regrets,
move into the future
  with a new perspective,
and appreciate the opportunity
  to take a second chance.

Acceptance means that when
  difficult times come into your life,
you'll find security again and comfort
  to relieve any pain.
You'll find new dreams, fresh hopes,
  and forgiveness of the heart.

Acceptance does not mean
    that you will always be perfect.
It simply means that
    you'll always overcome imperfection.

Acceptance is the road to peace —
    letting go of the worst,
holding on to the best,
    and finding the hope inside
that continues throughout life.

Acceptance is the heart's best defense,
    love's greatest asset,
and the easiest way to keep believing
    in yourself and others.

— Regina Hill

Don't Ever Stop Reaching and Growing

Don't be afraid of growing, changing, or living your life. No matter where you go or what you do, the true joy of life lies in the journey — not the destination. Search for your purpose, seek out your passions, and do what you love. It's not how long you live, but how you choose to live the days you are given, so choose to make the most of every opportunity you receive. Follow your dreams wherever they may lead, and live all the days of your life.

— Julie Ann Ford

It is never too late to be what you might have been.

— George Eliot (Mary Anne Evans)

When the road curves
to lead you into new discoveries...
let it take you.
When the wind pulls
    under your wings
and urges you on
        to greater heights...
            let it take you.
When the page you're on
    builds suspense, turn it –
for it will end happily.
Let it take you there.
The journey of life
    has no blueprints.
You find it as you grow
through prayer, joy,
pain, and love.
Keep moving on your path,
keep learning and trying
for the good and the best –
and it will take you there.

— Susan A. J. Lyttek

Ideals to Live By...

Learn from Your Mistakes

Life is like a giant puzzle.
Each of us has a picture in our minds
of how our lives will turn out.
We keep adding pieces, one at a time,
attempting to create that beautiful picture.
If one piece does not fit, we replace it
    with another.
We never get all the pieces in the right place
    on the first try.
It's all about experimenting until each piece
    fits together with the next.
Though our futures may not be clear
    or turn out exactly as we expected,
each of us has the strength inside to put
    the puzzle together.
We just have to look for the right pieces.
It may seem impossible, but keep striving.
Life's pieces have a way of falling into place
    when you least expect it.

— Renée M. Brtalik

Keep on beginning and failing. Each time you fail, start all over again, and you will grow stronger until you have accomplished a purpose – not the one you began with perhaps, but one you'll be glad to remember.

— Anne Sullivan

Setbacks and disappointments are something we all experience at one time or another. But if you refuse to believe in failure, you'll be able to find a way to open up all those doors that at one time you thought were closed to you forever. If you mark something down as a failure, then that's what it will be. But if you make up your mind to get the better of the situation, an experience that you once labeled as a failure can become another steppingstone toward happiness. So the next time something doesn't turn out exactly as you'd hoped, turn it around, be a fighter. Remember: it's the people who can turn a negative into a positive and bounce back who really get ahead in life.

— Mary Lou Retton

Be Enthusiastic About Your Life and Your Work

Enthusiasm is perhaps the greatest asset anyone can have. It is the key ingredient to success. You can have a wealth of skills, but if your heart is not in it, your work will reflect it. If you have enthusiasm, you will find the energy to acquire the necessary skills and draw to you all the people and support you need to succeed. Enthusiasm beats power, money, and influence.

— Joan Lunden

To be really alive means more than to be a moving, breathing, eating, drinking, and talking human creature. She who is actually alive finds the days too short for all the wonderful explorations which life offers....

She finds life itself a continual adventure, an unfolding panorama, with opportunities for pleasure and achievement at every turn.

— Ella Wheeler Wilcox

Purpose is knowing
what you want to do
and where you want to go in life.
Passion is letting nothing
stand in the way of getting there.
Passion is the fire inside your spirit,
the force that propels you forward,
and the determination
to make your dreams real.
Passion is the voice inside you
that says "Go for it!"

— Vickie M. Worsham

Happiness Comes from Within

The key to happiness
cannot be found in your
possessions.
You won't see it on a calendar
    of upcoming events.
It can't be given as a lavish gift
or even discovered within
    the greatest dreams.

The key to happiness is found
in the way you live each moment
and how you choose to express
    your feelings.
If you can lift your spirits
    high above circumstances;
if you can see life's sunny side;
if you can count your blessings...
then you have the key
that will open special doors for you.

The key to happiness lies within you.

— Barbara J. Hall

Happiness is a spirit of hope
that you carry within you
everywhere you go.
Happiness is the smile you share
and the truths you choose to live by.
It is a feeling of pleasure that makes you
want to be a part of all that surrounds you.
Happiness is allowing yourself
to experience life and all its wonders.
It is being yourself
and enjoying your uniqueness.
Happiness is not just one thing
but a collection of all things.
It is knowing that you matter
to those who know you.
Happiness is a state of mind.
Choose to be happy today!

— Deanna Beisser

Listen to Your Heart

You cannot listen
to what others
want you to do
You must listen
to yourself
Society
family
friends
and loved ones
do not know what
you must do
Only you know
and only you
can do what is
right for you

— Susan Polis Schutz

When you can look back on a day and find within it even one warm memory or a single touching story, you've paid attention to your heart. That's worth whatever time it took.

— Victoria Moran

The Heart Knows

Go where the heart
longs to go
Don't pay attention to the feet
that want to stay rooted

Go where the mind
wants to explore
Don't worry about the hands
that still want to hold on

Go where your gut
is fearful to go
Don't let your body
sit in one place

Go where your heart
knows it should go

— Natasha Josefowitz

Beauty Isn't Found
Just in Magazines

There is beauty
in so many unrecognized places.
It's a different beauty than
what you find in magazines,
where the faces all become the same
page after page.
Neither is it about shapes or fabrics
or cut and color.
Beauty is how you invite people
into your life and your heart no matter what;
it's when you laugh or cry with your whole self
just because that's how you feel.
Beauty is the way you move
when you think no one is watching
and you forget the shadows
of "should" and "supposed to."
Beauty is courage, energy, hope, and grace.
Beauty is you —
just the way you are.

— Sue Gillies-Bradley

A beautiful woman is any woman who
likes herself and loves other people.
She gives of herself
and cares about the happiness of others.
She walks through life
with a smile on her face and love in her heart.
She believes in being positive
and helps those who struggle.
She sings and dances to the music of each new day
and quietly gives thanks for all that she has.
She makes you feel comfortable
and allows you to be who you are.
She talks about her hopes and dreams
and passionately listens to yours.
She accepts herself for all that she is
and understands herself for all that she is not.
She is always trying to make her life better
and encourages others to do the same.
A beautiful woman may be a mother,
a sister, a wife,
a daughter, a best friend...
She's the little girl in every woman
who smiles because she just likes to smile
and embraces the world around her with love.

— Deanna Beisser

Appreciate Your Own
Self-Worth

If you know yourself well
and have developed a sense
of confidence in yourself
If you are honest with yourself
and honest with others
If you follow your heart
and adhere to your own truths
you are ready to share yourself
you are ready to set goals
you are ready to find happiness
And the more you love
and the more you give
and the more you feel
the more you will receive
from love
and the more you will receive
from life

— Susan Polis Schutz

Have Faith in Yourself

Within you...
unique qualities are engraved
in the heart of your soul,
each holding its own potential.
You are magnificent
in every sense of the word.
You were divinely created
and you have the artistry
to create an eloquent melody in life.

When you come to recognize
the marvelous soul you possess,
a new vision will unfold.
The real journey begins
when you find faith within yourself.

Walk forward and capture your dreams.
Hope for the unobtainable.
Reach for the unbelievable.
Strive for the undeniable.
Become the impossible.

— Leslie Neilson

Be Loving, Compassionate, and Kind

In our busy lives, we let life carry us away on a never-ending road filled with the responsibilities of a day-to-day existence.

We often forget that there is more along the way than just bills to pay, phone calls to return, and errands to run. There are people in our lives who need to be hugged, who need to be loved. There are people in our lives who need their accomplishments noticed and praised. We need to remember how fragile hearts can be, how quickly a soul can grow weary, how fast a spirit can break.

We forget that a heart is like a garden that needs to be tended to and nourished with what only another heart can give — love and appreciation, devotion and honesty.

— Tracia Gloudemans

Each of us has a few minutes a day or a few hours a week which we could donate to an old folks' home or a children's hospital ward. The elderly whose pillows we plump or whose water pitchers we refill may or may not thank us for our gift, but the gift is upholding the foundation of the universe. The children to whom we read simple stories may or may not show gratitude, but each boon we give strengthens the pillars of the world.

— Maya Angelou

Guard within yourself that treasure kindness. Know how to give without hesitation, how to lose without regret, how to acquire without meanness.

— George Sand (Aurore Dupin)

Find Something to Be Grateful for Every Day

Gratitude unlocks the fullness of life. Gratitude makes things right. It turns what we have into enough, and more. It turns denial into acceptance, chaos to order, confusion to clarity. It can turn a meal into a feast, a house into a home, a stranger into a friend. It turns problems into gifts, failures into successes, the unexpected into perfect timing, and mistakes into important events. It can turn an existence into a real life, and disconnected situations into important and beneficial lessons. Gratitude makes sense of our past, brings peace for today, and creates a vision for tomorrow.

— Melody Beattie

When to Be Thankful...

Be thankful when your blessings
far outnumber your reasons to cry;
when sorrow leaves and healing begins;
when those clouds overhead pass on by
and leave only sunshine in your life.

Be thankful when you think that you can't go on
but find the strength inside;
when that flicker of hope appears
to push away your doubts;
when everything has been deemed lost,
but you discover that what matters most
can never be taken from you —
because it rests inside your heart
warmly, safely, and secured with love.

Be thankful when someone whom you love
loves you in return;
when that one certain smile is turned your way;
and when you are singled out as someone
who is unique, cared for, and appreciated.

Be thankful for the blessings in your life
and count them often.
For when you welcome each one
with a grateful heart,
you'll find them continuing
to flow into your life every day.

— Barbara J. Hall

Perfection Is a Goal, Not a Reality

Perfection is a goal that can't be reached, but you can put your best into each effort, move through life with confidence, and learn to live with purpose.

Make it a priority to do all and be all you can. There will be mistakes along the way and some steps you may wish you hadn't taken, but there's something to be said for the learning process. It sharpens your wits and sheds light on your strengths. Sometimes it's good to fall short of a goal. It can lead to a brand new direction, a better way.

Don't ever give up. Don't ever stop trying. Never think you have to be perfect because nobody is. Just do what you do best. Keep moving with a purpose, and remember: it isn't only the happy endings that count, but also the joy we put into the journey.

— Barbara J. Hall

Sometimes you may
think that you
need to be perfect
that you cannot
make mistakes
At these times
you put so much
pressure on yourself
Try to realize
that you are
like everyone else —
capable of
reaching great potential
but not capable of
being perfect
Just do your best
and realize that
this is enough
Don't compare yourself
to anyone
Be happy to be
the wonderful
unique, very special
person that you are

— Susan Polis Schutz

Live Your Life Fully

Savor each moment presented to you. Make certain you've taken the time to watch the sun both rise and set and have allowed yourself a moment to enjoy the night light's game of hide-and-seek as the moon and stars peep out of the darkness.

Stop to appreciate the new blossom on a flower as its beauty unfolds and colors the earth.

Be silent and listen to the songs of nature as they greet you. The music of the birds and creatures around us is the gift of Mother Earth.

Smile at the people around you. Be aware that none of us exists within a vacuum and that who we are, what we do, and what we say will have an impact on someone every single day.

Search until you find something good about everyone you come in contact with during your day. It becomes easier with time and practice. Soon you'll see the positive in each person long before you find their faults, and somehow the weaknesses, even in yourself, will seem not so great.

Take a moment, even when you think there is none, to listen to the voice that speaks within you. Let it guide you toward your center and point you toward your future.

Learn to like who you are. We are none without our bad points, but don't allow yourself to focus only on those. Without day, there would be no night. Without cold, there would be no warmth. Without both the good and the bad in each of us, we would exist only as an image and not a real person. Allow yourself to be human — an ever-evolving person — but one with many facets.

Love fully. Love freely. And never regret the emotion. It is the most fragile, yet the strongest, of the threads that weave man's heart.

And, you've heard this before, never put it off. Never fail to tell someone special in your life that they are appreciated. It may not need to be said, but how gracefully it falls on the ears anyway, and how fully it embraces and warms the heart.

— Brenda Hager

Stay Positive!

We live in a very negative society,
and if we allow it,
negativity can feed our fears;
therefore, it's important
to keep a positive frame of mind.
This means that you may have to talk
to yourself sometimes to build yourself up.

Go ahead...
Boost yourself. Encourage yourself.
When faced with adversity,
   tell yourself:
"I can do this."
"I can accomplish this."
"I can do anything I want to."

— Bernice A. King

Remember, an obstacle is merely your personal strength in disguise, and if you believe you are capable of weathering the challenges that come your way, you can never fail. Have an upbeat attitude and feel good about what you're doing. The sky's the limit!

— T. L. Nash

You only get this one opportunity to be you. Use it to your advantage. Be proud of who you are; be proud of the person you become. Don't waste your precious energy on negative thoughts and images. Instead, open your heart and focus on all the beauty within and around you. It is there waiting to be seen. Life is waiting for you!

— Cindy Charlton

You Always Have Choices

You can choose to let
everything around you
pull you down into the depths
of self-doubt and anger
Or you can choose to find first
the good in yourself and those
that surround you.

You can choose to see
only the negative in the
situation that presents itself
Or you can look for the positive
things in all your endeavors.

You can choose to let
the dark part of
your soul take over and tear
at your confidence
Or you can choose to see
the light, the brightness
in who you are and
find comfort in yourself.

You can let fear drive wedges
between those you love and yourself
Or you can find the strength
and the faith to cherish those
relationships and hold fast to them.

You can choose to live
your life fully and honestly,
letting each person you meet
know their worth,
even when you don't
always agree with them.

You can choose to remove yourself
from those situations you cannot control
without losing your sense of purpose.

You can choose to value all life
without agreeing with all opinions.

You can choose to be strong.
You can choose to be loving.
You can choose to be true to yourself.

You can choose to live
fully and without regret.

— Brenda Hager

Leave the World a Little Better Than You Found It

It's terribly important at every age to somehow leap out of the constriction of one's own mind and get involved in something larger than oneself. Do whatever you want to do. Write a poem, plant a rosebush, go to India, be kind to other people.... Find your place and your cause and something besides yourself to get passionate about. Go out and make the world work. Take any one thing that needs to be done in the world and add one little bit to it, and that will pay off immeasurably, mostly in terms of helping yourself.

— Sally Jessy Raphael

In times of doubt, remember...
When you toss
even the tiniest of pebbles
into the ocean,
ripples do form.
Small, radiating circles
that bring waves of change
to the flowing current of the water.
Within the ocean of humanity,
you are the pebble.
You have the ability to create the waves
and bring change to every life
you touch.

— J. Marie Larson

Remember All That It Means to Be a Woman

A woman is a person of strength. Yet it is in her weakest moments that she is strongest.

A woman is a person of intuition. She can "fine tune" her inner voice and find that place of wisdom within her soul.

A woman is a person of independence. She stands proudly on her own, knowing she can always count on herself.

A woman is a person of trust. Confide in her and she'll lock it in her heart forever. Betray her trust and you've lost a true friend.

A woman is a person of vulnerability.
   She sees the world with a
   kaleidoscope of passion, inviting
   others to see beyond the black
   and white.

A woman is a person of emotion.
   She pours it in different quantities,
   but never runs out.

A woman is a person of gratitude.
   She never takes for granted the
   beauty of human generosity.

A woman is a person of wisdom and
   maturity. Through her maturity, she
   gains wisdom — and with that
   wisdom, she matures.

A woman is a person of awareness
   and spirit. She flows with the
   universe... to be where she is
   meant to be.

                    — Debbie Burton-Peddle

You're Never Too Old
to Make a Difference

With the passage of years come the gifts
of wisdom, of experience, of respect.
The changing of the seasons assigns a deeper purpose
to life... a wider sense of its truest meaning.
It teaches through trial and error not just to live
for oneself, but for others as well.
It lifts off all past restrictions with the challenge
that you can still do everything you want...
if you only put your mind to it.
It encourages you to keep your brain active,
to keep your thoughts positive.
It laughs a lot, plays a lot, loves a lot.
As the hands of time tick on...
moments become more precious,
not because the hours are moving by more quickly,
but because you've gained a higher sense
of how truly wonderful life is.

— Linda E. Knight

We all become different people
as we grow older,
with different hopes and dreams,
goals and achievements,
memories and feelings.
No one can ever say that, as a person,
they are all they can be,
for it is then that they
have stopped growing from within.
We must continue to grow,
to dream,
to make new memories,
and to do whatever gives us peace
within ourselves.

                  — Shirley Vander Pol

Look for a Little Happiness in Each Day

Live in the moment
and let your heart believe.
Search for the hidden treasures
   in every day.
Fill your life with happiness
and keep your eyes on the goal.
Take a moment to come home
   to your heart
every single day.
It's the little things
that make a great big difference,
so take time out to play and
laugh a little every day.
Fill your sky with sunbeams
and your heart with song.

Your dreams are out there
   looking for you.
Celebrate your blessings
and count your strengths.
Let hope be your guide
and faith be your wings.
Open your eyes to
   each day's promise;
open the dawn and
   welcome your dreams.
Tomorrow is of your making...
stretch your limits and grow!

— Linda E. Knight

Don't Let Anything Stand
in the Way of Your Dreams

Catch the star that holds your destiny —
the one that forever twinkles
within your heart
Take advantage of precious opportunities
while they still sparkle before you
Always believe that your ultimate goal
is attainable as long as you
commit yourself to it
Though barriers may sometimes
stand in the way of your dreams
remember that your destiny is hiding behind them
Accept the fact that not everyone
is going to approve of the choices you make
but have faith in your judgment
Catch the star that twinkles in your heart
and it will lead you to your destiny's path

Follow that pathway and uncover the
sweet sunrises that await you
Take pride in your accomplishments
as they are steppingstones to your dreams
Understand that you may make mistakes
but don't let them discourage you
Value your capabilities and talents
for they are what make you truly unique
The greatest gifts in life are not purchased
but acquired through hard work and determination
Find the star that twinkles in your heart
for you are capable of making
your brightest dreams come true
Give your hopes everything you've got
and you will catch the star
that holds your destiny

— Shannon M. Lester

Above All Else,
Believe in Yourself

As the dawn of each morning
peers into your life,
there lies a path to follow.
Delicate whispers can be heard
if you listen to the sound of your heart
and the voice that speaks within you.

If you listen closely to your soul,
you will become aware of your dreams
that are yet to unfold.
You will discover that there lies within you
a voice of confidence and strength
that will prompt you to seek a journey
and live a dream.

Within the depths of your mind,
the purpose and direction of your life
can be determined by listening intently
to the knowledge that you already possess.
Your heart, mind, and soul
are the foundation
of your success and happiness.

In the still of each passing moment,
you will come to understand that
you are capable of reaching a higher destiny.
When you come to believe
in all that you are
and all that you can become,
there will be no cause for doubt.
Believe in your heart, for it offers hope.
Believe in your mind, for it offers direction.
Believe in your soul, for it offers strength.
But above all else... believe in yourself.

— Leslie Neilson

ACKNOWLEDGMENTS

We gratefully acknowledge the permission granted by the following authors and authors' representatives to reprint poems or excerpts from their publications.

PrimaDonna Entertainment Corp. for "Take Time Each Day to Remember What's Important" and "Have at Least One True Friend" by Donna Fargo. Copyright © 2001, 2006 by PrimaDonna Entertainment Corp. All rights reserved.

Tanya Shubin for "Be the Person You Are Meant to Be." Copyright © 2006 by Tanya Shubin. All rights reserved.

Barbara J. Hall for "Worry Never Solves Anything," "Happiness Comes from Within," "When to Be Thankful…," and "Perfection Is a Goal, Not a Reality." Copyright © 2006 by Barbara J. Hall. All rights reserved.

Dana Smith-Mansell for "Sometimes we move the earth…." Copyright © 2006 by Dana Smith-Mansell. All rights reserved.

Dena DiIaconi for "Measure Success in Your Own Way." Copyright © 2006 by Dena DiIaconi. All rights reserved.

Conari Press, an imprint of Red Wheel/Weiser, Newburyport, MA and San Francisco, CA, for "It's so easy for women…" from WOMEN'S WORK IS NEVER DONE by BJ Gallagher. Copyright © 2006 by BJ Gallagher. All rights reserved.

Faith Tomassacci for "Where Love Grows." Copyright © 2006 by Faith Tomassacci. All rights reserved.

Julie Ann Ford for "Don't be afraid of growing…." Copyright © 2006 by Julie Ann Ford. All rights reserved.

Renée M. Brtalik for "Learn from Your Mistakes." Copyright © 2006 by Renée M. Brtalik. All rights reserved.

Broadway Books, a division of Random House, Inc., for "Setbacks and disappointments are…" from MARY LOU RETTON'S GATEWAY TO HAPPINESS by Mary Lou Retton. Copyright © 2000 by MLR Entertainment, Inc. and Momentum Partners, Inc. All rights reserved. And for for "Stay Positive!" from HARD QUESTIONS, HEART ANSWERS by Bernice A. King. Copyright © 1996 by Bernice A. King. All rights reserved.

McGraw-Hill for "Enthusiasm is perhaps the greatest…" from WAKE-UP CALLS by Joan Lunden. Copyright © 2001 by New Life Entertainment, Inc. All rights reserved.

Vickie M. Worsham for "Purpose is knowing what you want…." Copyright © 2006 by Vickie M. Worsham. All rights reserved.

Deanna Beisser for "Happiness is a spirit of hope" and "A beautiful woman is any woman…." Copyright © 2006 by Deanna Beisser. All rights reserved.

HarperCollins Publishers and Victoria Moran for "When you can look back…" from CREATING A CHARMED LIFE by Victoria Moran. Copyright © 1999 by Victoria Moran. All rights reserved.

Natasha Josefowitz for "The Heart Knows" from TOO WISE TO WANT TO BE YOUNG AGAIN. Copyright © 1995 by Natasha Josefowitz. All rights reserved.

Sue Gillies-Bradley for "Beauty Isn't Found Just in Magazines." Copyright © 2006 by Sue Gillies-Bradley. All rights reserved.

Leslie Neilson for "Have Faith in Yourself." Copyright © 2006 by Leslie Neilson. All rights reserved.

Random House, Inc., and Virago Press, a division of Time Warner Book Group Company UK, for "Each of us has a few minutes…" from WOULDN'T TAKE NOTHING FOR MY JOURNEY NOW by Maya Angelou. Copyright © 1993 by Maya Angelou. All rights reserved.

Ballantine Books, a division of Random House, Inc., for "Gratitude unlocks the fullness of life" from GRATITUDE by Melody Beattie. Copyright © 1992 by Hazelden Foundation. All rights reserved.

Brenda Hager for "Live Your Life Fully" and "You Always Have Choices." Copyright © 2006 by Brenda Hager. All rights reserved.

T. L. Nash for "Remember, an obstacle is merely…." Copyright © 2006 by T. L. Nash. All rights reserved.

Cindy Charlton for "You only get this one opportunity…." Copyright © 2006 by Cindy Charlton. All rights reserved.

St. Martin's Press for "It's terribly important at every age…" by Sally Jessy Raphael from WHAT WE KNOW SO FAR, compiled and edited by Beth Benatovich. Copyright © 1995 by Beth Benatovich Berenson. All rights reserved.

J. Marie Larson for "In times of doubt…." Copyright © 2006 by J. Marie Larson. All rights reserved.

Debbie Burton-Peddle for "What It Means to Be a Woman." Copyright © 2006 by Debbie Burton-Peddle. All rights reserved.

Linda E. Knight for "You're Never Too Old to Make a Difference" and "Look for a Little Happiness in Each Day." Copyright © 2006 by Linda E. Knight. All rights reserved.

A careful effort has been made to trace the ownership of selections used in this anthology in order to obtain permission to reprint copyrighted material and give proper credit to the copyright owners. If any error or omission has occurred, it is completely inadvertent, and we would like to make corrections in future editions provided that written notification is made to the publisher:

BLUE MOUNTAIN ARTS, INC., P.O. Box 4549, Boulder, Colorado 80306.